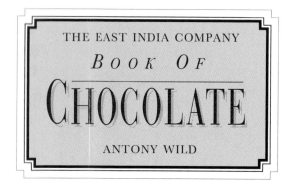

THE EAST INDIA COMPANY
BOOK OF
CHOCOLATE

ANTONY WILD

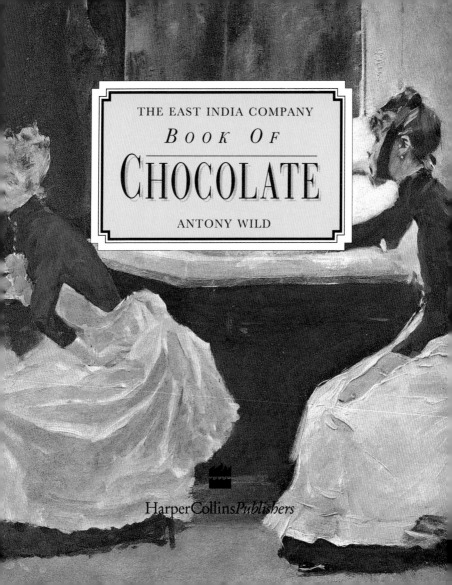

THE EAST INDIA COMPANY

BOOK OF

CHOCOLATE

ANTONY WILD

HarperCollins*Publishers*

First published in 1995 by
HarperCollins*Publishers*, London

Text © Antony Victor Wild 1995

Antony Wild asserts the moral right to
be identified as the author of this work

Commissioning Editor: Polly Powell
Editor: Lisa Eaton
Cover Design: Ian Butterworth
Designer: Rachel Smyth
Picture Researcher: Lisa Eaton

The publishers and author would like to thank
Nicky and Alan Porter, Robert Baldwin, Drew Smith
and David Hutton.

**A catalogue record for this book is
available from the British Library**

ISBN 0 00 412774 9

Colour reproduction by Colourscan, Singapore
Printed and bound in Spain
by Artes Graficas Toledo, S.A.
D.L.TO: 820-1995

Contents

The East India Company

The Armorial Bearings of the Company of Merchants of London
trading into the East Indies granted by Garter and Clarenceux
Kings of Arms in 1600, and as borne and used until 1709

*F*ounded by the Royal Charter of Queen Elizabeth I in 1600, the East India Company was the single most powerful economic force that the world has ever seen. Its influence reached out to all continents, and the consequences of its actions, both great and small, are the very fabric of history. The Company created British India; founded Hong Kong and Singapore; caused the Boston Tea Party; employed Captain Kidd to combat piracy; held Napoleon captive; and made the fortune of Elihu Yale who founded his famous university with the proceeds.

The Stars and Stripes was inspired by its flag, its shipyards provided the model for St Petersburg, its London chapel set the pattern for New England churches, its administration still forms the basis of Indian bureaucracy, and its corporate structure was the earliest example of a joint stock company. It introduced tea to Britain and India, woollens to Japan, chintzes to America, spices to the West Indies, opium to China, porcelain to Russia, and polo to Persia. It had its own armies, navies, currencies, and territories as diverse as the tiny Spice Island, Pulo Run – which was later exchanged for

Manhattan – to the 'Jewel in the Crown', India itself. As *The Times* newspaper reported in 1874 when the Company was finally absorbed by the Crown: 'It is just as well to record that it accomplished a work such as in the whole history of the human race no other Company ever attempted and, as such, is ever likely to attempt in the years to come.'

East India House

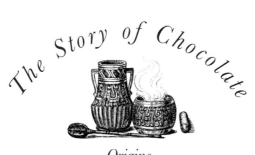

The Story of Chocolate

Origins

*C*hocolate comes from cocoa, which is produced from the fruit-like pod of the tropical cocoa tree. The chocolate-making process as we understand it today was only invented relatively recently. Up until the middle of the 19th century chocolate was mostly consumed as a beverage, similar to what we now call cocoa. This drink was frequently described as bitter, and often mixed with spices such as chilli peppers. Its taste bore little resemblance to most of today's chocolate bars, although you can still taste some of this pleasantly bitter flavour in the very highest quality chocolate.

The story of cocoa begins with the ancient kingdoms of Central America. The Aztecs and Mayans used cocoa as a vital part of the many ceremonies which punctuated their lives, including christenings, weddings and funerals. Reflecting the importance of chocolate in their cultures, cocoa planters had their own god, Ekchuah, to whom a dog bearing a cocoa-coloured spot was ritually slaughtered. Cocoa was given to brave warriors as a reward in the form of a drink called *xocolatl,* and duly withheld from the cowardly with the injunction: 'He will not receive tobacco. He will not drink chocolate; he will not eat fine foods.' Indeed cocoa beans were of such value that they were also used as currency, prompting a contemporary historian, Peter Martyr, to describe cocoa as: 'Blessed money, which exempts its possessors from avarice, as it cannot long be hoarded or hidden underground.'

It was Christopher Columbus who first brought cocoa to the attention of the West, when in 1502 he returned from Nicaragua with some cocoa beans to present to his patron, King Ferdinand of Spain (who was profoundly

Indians making offerings of cocoa and fruit, 16th century

unimpressed). In fact, it was the extraordinary success of the Spanish conqueror Hernán Cortés in penetrating the Aztec kingdom of Montezuma, some 20 years later, which eventually gave rise to a sustained European interest in chocolate.

Aztec astrologers had fixed upon the year 1519 for the return of their mythical plumed serpent god Quetzcoatl, who had, among other things, been credited with introducing cocoa to the Aztecs before being tricked out of his powers and exiled. When Cortés and his small party landed on the Mexican coast in 1519, therefore, the Aztecs mistook him for their returning god, giving Cortés an easy passage through to the Aztec capital. Upon his arrival Cortés was treated with the customary hospitality, including chocolate to drink – giving rise to the ancient Aztec tongue twister 'Quetzacoatl drinks *xocolatl*'. Only too late did Montezuma realize that the Spanish adventurer was not the expected plumed serpent god, and by 1521 the Emperor was dead, his civilization laid to waste, and his capital, Tenochtitlán, the centre of New Spain.

In 1528 Cortés returned to Spain, taking chocolate and the Aztec chocolate-making implements with him. He introduced chocolate to the Spanish Court, where their own version of this new drink became extremely fashionable.

The Spanish conqueror Hernán Cortés marvelled at the fact that: 'One cup of this precious drink allows a man to walk a whole day without taking nourishment.'

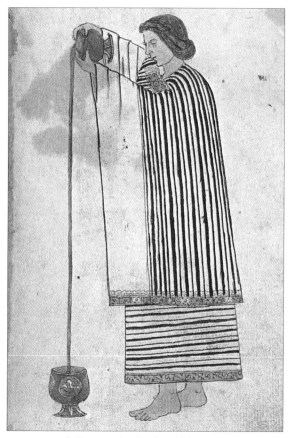

Indian preparing chocolate, 16th century

What's in a name?

As with the name of many other foods, the origin of cocoa's name is the subject of some controversy. The botanical name for the cocoa tree is Theobroma cacao *– 'cocoa, food of the Gods'. The tree, the bean and the powder extracted from it are all termed cocoa, which was originally spelt 'cacao' and is still sometimes spelt 'cocao'. To add to the confusion, the word chocolate itself appears to be derived from the Aztec word* xocolatl, *which means 'bitter water', while the Italians also claim that the suffix derives from their word* latte, *meaning 'milk'. This would imply that all chocolate is milk chocolate, which is not the case.*

Aztecs roasting and preparing chocolate

The chocolate trade

Initially introduced to Europe by the Spanish in the 16th century, it was some time before the fashion for chocolate drinking spread further afield. In the late 16th century, Jews driven out of Spain settled in Bayonne in south-west France and introduced chocolate to the region, which has remained

Drinking chocolate in France, 17th century

CHOICE
RECIPES

REG. U.S.
PAT. OFF.

COMPLIMENTS OF
WALTER BAKER & CO., LTD
DORCHESTER, MASS.
ESTABLISHED 1780.

*Belgian silver
chocolate pot, 1686*

a centre for chocolate making to this day. Elsewhere in France, chocolate drinking was brought over from the Spanish to the French court when Anne of Austria married Louis XIII in 1615, and Maria Theresa married Louis XIV in 1660. In Italy, the explorer Antonio Carletti introduced cocoa to the country in 1606 on return from his travels in Central America. By the end of the century the chocolate houses of Florence and Venice were renowned.

After 1650 chocolate began to be sold in all the principal cities of Europe, firstly in the then burgeoning coffee houses, and later in dedicated chocolate houses. In Switzerland chocolate was first noted in 1697, when the Mayor of Zurich discovered it on a visit to Brussels, and the first chocolate factory in Germany was founded in 1756. To service a rapid increase in popularity, chocolate pots and cups of silver or porcelain were soon being made all over Europe.

Needless to say, the governments of the day seized upon the import of chocolate as a potential source of revenue, and swingeing taxes were imposed. By the time of the reign of George III of England, for example, the East India Company had to pay two shillings in tax per pound of cocoa imported.

A similar pattern was repeated all over Europe, inevitably leading to the adulteration of cocoa and a great increase in smuggling.

America was surprisingly late in discovering the pleasures of chocolate, and the first factory – the still-famous Walter Baker Company – was not established until 1765. The Ghirardelli Californian Chocolate Manufactory was set up in 1856, developing out of a grocer's business introduced to serve the Gold Rush. To this day Ghirardelli Square remains a San Francisco landmark, and the eponymous chocolate a firm American favourite.

Montezuma, ruler of the fabulously wealthy Aztec kingdom, was served chocolate in golden cups before visiting his many wives.

Recipe for Aztec Chocolate Drink

Bring 17fl oz (500ml) of water to the boil in a small saucepan. Mix in thoroughly a pinch of powdered chilli pepper, a pinch of turmeric, a small pinch of powdered ginger, a sachet of vanilla-flavoured sugar and five teaspoons of honey, and bring back to the boil. Remove from the heat and stir in 3oz (75g) of cocoa paste which has been chopped into little pieces. Keep stirring until well mixed and whisk vigorously before serving.

The cocoa bean

The cocoa tree is an evergreen indigenous to the rain forests of Central America, but is now cultivated in the tropical Americas, the Caribbean, West Africa, Madagascar, the Philippines and the East Indies. The tree needs plenty of rain, consistent warmth and some shade, and left wild it will grow to a height of 40 feet (12 metres). There are two main varieties: the 'Criollo', which produces the best quality cocoa, and the lower quality 'Forastero', which is more robust and

The cocoa harvest on the island of Sao Tomé, c. 1935

productive. A hybrid of 'Criollo', the 'Trinitario', is now grown throughout the Caribbean.

Each tree produces many blossoms, but only about 50 pods for the biannual harvest. A cocoa pod is roughly 8 inches (20 centimetres) long, 4 inches (10 centimetres) in diameter, and contains around 40 beans. The pods turn golden yellow when ripe, and are then cut from the trees by machete, and split open to reveal the beans. These are removed from their surrounding pulp and spread out on banana leaves.

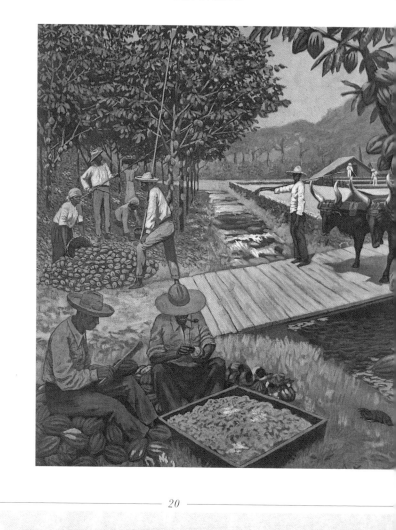

Extracting cocoa beans from the pods, c. 1894

Over the next six days the beans ferment, the outside eventually oxidizing and turning pale brown. This is when much of the characteristic aroma and flavour of chocolate develops. Afterwards the beans are dried under canopies to protect them from the rain. Once properly fermented and dried, they are weighed and graded at a central location, and the farmer is paid for his produce. An individual tree may produce only 10 pounds (4.5 kilos) of these dried cocoa beans a year. Finally, the beans are put into sacks, ready for shipping to different countries to be turned into cocoa powder or chocolate.

From bean to bar

The manufacturing process begins with the roasting of the beans in a large revolving cylinder at a temperature of about 284°F (140°C). The longer the beans stay in the roaster, the darker their colour. The finer flavours of the 'Criollo' beans are best preserved in a medium roast, while the coarser flavours of the 'Forastero' variety are partly obscured by a dark roast.

Once roasted, the brittle shell of the bean is then cracked open and the 'winnowing' process begins. This is where the brittle shell is blown away, leaving behind the heavier centre, the 'nib'. This is the most important part of the bean. The 'nibs' are ground through a series of rollers whose pressure and heat cause the cocoa butter to melt and to separate from

French chocolate factory

the cocoa 'liquor' or 'mass'. This separation process was invented in the early 19th century by a Dutchman named Van Houten. It completely revolutionized chocolate making, removing the need to add maize or flour to absorb the fatty cocoa butter which floated on top of the drink.

Next the cocoa 'liquor' is mixed with ground sugar, vanilla and some of the cocoa butter, in readiness for the 'conching' process. (To make milk chocolate, powdered, evaporated or condensed milk can be added just before this stage.) Once the chocolate has been further rolled into a smooth paste, it is then put into the 'conching' machine (invented by Rudolfe Lindt in

prenez du Cacao
Van Houten

1880, and named after its shell-like shape). Inside this machine the paste is gently ground between granite rollers for anything up to 100 hours for the very finest chocolates. For extra smoothness, more cocoa butter may be introduced.

Rolling the chocolate, Italy, 19th century

'Conching' rids the chocolate of any residual grittiness, and also helps reduce bitterness. The result is a silky smooth texture beloved by chocolate lovers the world over.

Before it is ready for packing the chocolate must be 'tempered', a gentle warming process which realigns the crystalline structure of the cocoa butter, giving the chocolate a shiny appearance and a good 'snap' when broken. It is then poured into moulds which form the blocks, bars or finished chocolate sweets. The French word *couverture* describes the chocolate which is produced for use by professional confectioners. In France the word is very specific, and means that the chocolate must contain at least 32 per cent cocoa butter; elsewhere the word *couverture* can be applied to simple cooking chocolate.

Packing chocolates, early 20th century

Recipe for Fail-safe Chocolate Brownies

Cream 4oz (125g) of butter or margarine and 8oz (250g) of soft brown sugar together, until the mixture is light and fluffy. Add two eggs, beating thoroughly. Sift together 3oz (75g) of flour, 1½oz (40g) of cocoa powder and half a teaspoon of baking powder, and stir into the creamed mixture until well blended. Spread in a buttered swiss roll tin (jelly roll pan) of the size 7 x 11in (178 x 279mm). Bake in the centre of a moderate oven (Gas 4, 350°F, 180°C) for 30 minutes, and then cut into squares while still warm, dusting with caster (superfine) sugar.

Blooming chocolate

Anyone familiar with chocolate may occasionally have seen a dull white 'bloom' on their shiny brown chocolate, and wondered whether it is harmful. There are, in fact, two types of 'bloom'. The first is caused by too much heat, when the cocoa butter crystals melt and come to the surface. Upon solidifying they form white crystals, and also give the chocolate a slightly gritty texture. This problem can be cured by 'retempering' the chocolate. The second type is more serious and is caused by moisture, often when the finished chocolate is stored in damp conditions. The sugar in the chocolate absorbs the moisture from the surrounding air, causing the sugar crystals to reform on the surface and making the chocolate inedible. Chocolate should be stored in cool, dry conditions. A refrigerator is not ideal because it contains moisture, and the chocolate may also absorb odours from other foods.

Samuel Pepys refers in his diary to the time when he woke with an almighty hangover after the coronation of Charles II and 'so rose, and went with Mr Creed to drink our morning draft, which he did give me in chocolate to settle my stomach.'

Simon Bolívar, who liberated South America from the yoke of Spanish imperialism, was the son of a cocoa planter and a planter himself.

Beautifying butter

Cocoa butter is unique among fats in that, while it is solid at temperatures up to 91.4°F (33°C), it melts at 93.2°F (34°C) – just below blood temperature at 98.6°F (37°C). As a result of this, it is highly sought after in the cosmetics industry for the manufacture of lipstick and other beauty products. Chocolate manufacturers can therefore demand very high prices for their cocoa butter, and some find it more economical to replace the butter required for chocolate manufacture with other 'enhancers', such as oils derived from nuts or palm. While this may be healthy for the profits of the manufacturers, it has a detrimental effect on the taste of the chocolate, tending to leave a greasy aftertaste. When buying chocolate, therefore, try to avoid anything with animal or vegetable fats listed on the label.

Horace Walpole, a member of the eminent British political family and writer of Gothick novels, took chocolate with him on 'The Grand Tour', and sarcastically named a gathering of more than half a dozen ladies a 'ciocolata'.

Goethe, German poet and playwright, also took supplies of chocolate with him on his travels, including on an extended visit to Switzerland in 1797, where chocolate was not yet produced.

Tasting chocolate

Chocolate is now a worldwide industry, supporting a host of major brands for whom the consistency of flavour is vital. This consistency can be achieved only through the skilled blending and roasting of the cocoa beans. Ultimately it is down to the human palate to determine whether the cocoa is of the required quality, and to even out seasonal and geographical variations. Equally, at the gourmet end of the chocolate market, the skill and experience of chocolate tasters help to ensure the sublime flavours we crave. The final product is monitored just as carefully – legend has it that every morning a Mars Bar from the previous day's production is brought into the chairman's office on a silver tray for his approval.

Tasters take a small chunk of chocolate and allow it to melt on the tongue in order to assess various qualities.

Appearance – The chocolate should be smooth and shiny, with no hint of 'bloom' or air bubbles. Generally, the more red-brown its colour, the better the chocolate.

Snap – The crystalline structure of the cocoa butter in well-made chocolate should give it a distinctive clean 'snap' when broken.

Flavour – As with all tasting disciplines, chocolate tasting has its own vocabulary with particular characteristics sought out and described. The characteristics of the finest 'Criollo'

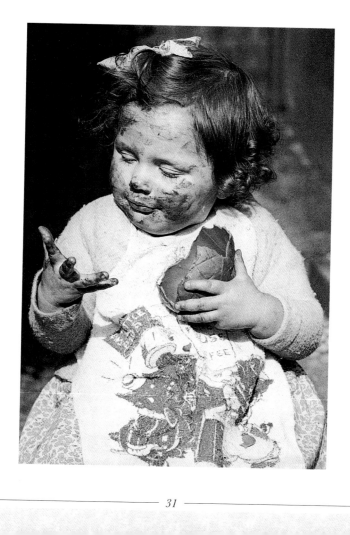

cocoa beans, for example, are manifested in the chocolate as a delicious fruitiness and acidity. If natural vanilla is used as an additional flavouring, the chocolate will have a light, sweet flavour, whereas artificial vanilla can be identified in the slightly cloying aroma of the chocolate. Similarly, the addition of too much sugar can overwhelm the delicate flavour of a good quality chocolate.

Touch – Cocoa butter melts at just below blood temperature, so if chocolate starts to melt after being held in the hand for a few seconds it is a sign that the cocoa butter content is high.

Recipe for Chocolate Mousse

Mix two tablespoons of coffee into a cup of water, before slowly melting 7oz (200g) of dark chocolate (at least 60 per cent cocoa solids) in a double boiler. Add the coffee and one and a half teaspoons of rum to the chocolate. Mix in half a grated orange rind. Separate four eggs, whisk the yolks and then add these to the chocolate mixture. Add a pinch of salt. Beat the egg whites until stiff, and add the mixture to them. Spoon the mousse into a bowl before grating another quarter of an orange rind on top. Leave to set in the refrigerator for at least six hours before serving.

Drinking Chocolate

How the drink was made

The Aztecs made *xocolatl* by roasting dried cocoa beans in pans and grinding them to form a paste which was then mixed with water. This was beaten with a *molinillo* – a wooden whisk which was an essential piece of chocolate-making equipment (*see above*). Maize was added to absorb the cocoa butter and, at this stage, it was also possible to let the mixture dry into crude bars of chocolate, in preparation for the final drink. Chillis and aniseed were sometimes added and, when the habit was first taken up by Europeans, cinnamon, cloves and logwood were also included. Sugar and vanilla, the vital ingredients of modern chocolate, were introduced when the fashion for drinking chocolate spread from Spain to the rest of Europe in the early 17th century. The *molinillo* still played an important role in the preparation of the drink, and its aristocratic patrons employed staff dedicated to this task. Indeed, when Maria Theresa married Louis XIV she brought her *Molina* with her – a maid whose sole task it was to make her mistress's chocolate. As Despina complains in Mozart's *Cosi fan tutti:* 'What an abominable life a lady's maid leads! ... I've been beating chocolate for half an hour, now it's ready, and is it my lot to stand and smell it with a dry mouth?'

It was said of Maria Theresa, wife of Louis XIV: 'Chocolate and the King are her only passions.' She presented Louis with some chocolate in a casket as an engagement gift.

Sherlock Holmes drank chocolate for breakfast.

'A cup of chocolate' by Sir John Lavery

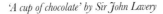

Vanilla – a vital ingredient

The use of vanilla as the key flavouring for chocolate is so well established that it is difficult to imagine how it would taste without it. Vanilla was actively cultivated by the Aztecs, which accounts for its use in the early chocolate recipes, and indeed its production remained a monopoly of Mexico until 1841. Today its cultivation has now spread to other parts of Central America, Madagascar and Réunion. As a result of the lengthy and complex 'curing' process involved, its production is costly. This high price led to the development of a synthetic vanillin (the main flavour element of natural vanilla), and these inferior synthetics now make up around 90 per cent of the world's trade. Good chocolate, however, should always be flavoured with natural vanilla, which is still much in demand in France, Germany and the United States.

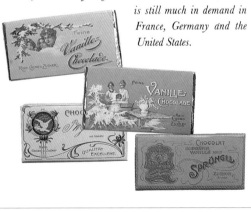

Chocolate houses

By the middle of the 17th century drinking chocolate was popular all over Europe, and enjoyed mostly in chocolate houses. In London the most famous was White's Chocolate House, opened in 1693 by an Italian immigrant. White's, along with another London chocolate house, The Cocoa Tree, later developed into men's clubs.

Although not such a hotbed of seditious politics as The Cocoa Tree, White's was one of the main haunts for men and women of fashion in the 18th century. Home to chocolate drinking and vicious gossip, White's was also <u>the</u> place in London to gamble, with vast fortunes being won and lost at the card table.

White's Chocolate House, 18th century

Chocolate for breakfast in France, c. 1800

A sweeter drink

As we have seen, chocolate was almost exclusively a drink, which gradually evolved over the years from a savoury to a sweet beverage. The technique for making drinking chocolate with milk was not invented until the 17th century, by a distinguished English surgeon, Sir Hans Sloane. The secret of this process eventually found its way to the Cadbury brothers, and became the foundation of their success. However, until the invention of Van Houten's cocoa press in the early 19th century, one problem remained – how to get rid of the excess cocoa butter which floated on the top of the liquid. At a stroke, this invention made possible modern solid chocolate manufacturing, as well as improving the drink itself. The inventive Van Houten was also responsible for 'dutching', a process involving the treatment, under heat and pressure, of the cocoa 'nibs' with an alkali such as potash. This improves both the flavour and colour of the cocoa, and enables the powder produced to dissolve easily in water or milk. Thus modern cocoa was born.

Recipe for French Chocolate Crème Pâtissière
Pour 18fl oz (0.5 litre) of milk and a vanilla pod split lengthways into a pan with 2oz (50g) of caster (superfine) sugar. Bring to the boil, remove from the heat and allow to infuse for 15 minutes. Beat six egg yolks together with another 3½oz (100g) of caster sugar and whisk until it has whitened and doubled in volume. Slowly add 1½oz (40g) of cornflour (cornstarch) and 1½oz (40g) of plain flour together. Bring the milk back to the boil, and remove the vanilla pod. Pour half the milk slowly into the mixture, stirring vigorously, and pour back into the rest of the milk. Leave on a low heat for about five minutes, whisking to ensure that it thickens evenly. Warm 5oz (150g) of dark chocolate pieces with a spoonful of water in a double saucepan. Add this and three spoonfuls of unsweetened pure cocoa powder to the mixture. Allow to cool. This can be used for traditional French éclairs and soufflés.

The enlightened capitalists

Among the great beverages of the world, chocolate alone has attracted enterprising businessmen with a philanthropic streak. In England many of the great chocolate makers were Quakers, a tolerant and peace-loving, if rather austere sect, founded by George Fox. These included the Frys, the Rowntrees, the Terrys and the Cadburys. Disbarred by their faith from the professions, and with a wish to help the poor, they chose cocoa as a commodity because they believed it to be a nourishing drink and a healthy alternative to gin. The model villages they established to house their workers, and the enlightened health and education schemes they introduced, had a tremendous effect on social thinking. Descendants of these families were also instrumental in radical prison reforms and the care of the mentally ill. Indeed

to this day the Joseph Rowntree Trust is one of the most influential research bodies into poverty and social deprivation in Britain.

Cocoa label, c. 1830

Afternoon chocolate, 1905

The attraction to English philanthropists of chocolate making was mirrored in the United States by the activities of Milton Hershey. In 1900, he set up a chocolate factory in Pennsylvania, a state founded by persecuted English Quakers. Hersheyville, his model village, emulated the enlightened regimes already in place at Bourneville, the Cadburys' model factory and village, and York, home of the Rowntrees and Terrys. Hershey's chocolate was used as an essential part of the rations of American soldiers fighting in the Second World War, and is still extremely successful. Meanwhile in France, the Chocolat Menier works at Noisel gave rise to a similar model village for its workers.

The French author, Voltaire, frequently drank chocolate with his friend Frederick the Great of Prussia.

Spanish chocolate service

Death by Chocolate

The fanciful name of this famous chocolate cake conjures up images of an exquisite death caused by overindulgence. There are, however, several tales of passion and intrigue in which chocolate is the cause of death. One such story concerns the Bishop of Chiapas in Mexico, who banned the ladies of his diocese from drinking chocolate in his cathedral, a habit which helped sustain them during his interminable sermons. Revenge was theirs, however, when an irate group of ladies persuaded the Bishop's page to add poison to his chocolate – a pleasure in which he freely indulged himself – and he died an agonising death. In Mexico to this day those seeking to impose their views on others are warned: 'Beware the chocolate of Chiapas!'

The Court of Louis XIII of France was quick to take up the fashion for chocolate drinking which was sweeping the royal houses of Europe. One particular courtier developed a special appreciation of the finer points of chocolate making. True to the fashion of a country still equally dedicated to the arts of food and lovemaking, he was also something of a rake, who had compromised the honour of a lady of quality. Inviting him to take chocolate with her, she poisoned his cup. With true Gallic flair he fell dying into her arms declaring: 'The chocolate would have been better if you had added a little more sugar; the poison gives it a bitter flavour.'

The World of Chocolate

Chocolate today

*N*owadays, the vast majority of chocolate is consumed in the form of bars, candies, cakes and other sweets. First made in the early 19th century, eating-chocolate has assumed a significant role in modern life, whether as Easter eggs commemorating a religious event, or boxes of chocolates expressing love. Today chocolate is consumed as a delicious solid food, a part of our everyday lives.

Indeed, chocolate is now loved the world over. As one would expect from the importance of its chocolate industries, the Swiss lead the world's consumption table, consuming nearly 22 pounds (10 kilos) per head each year. Belgium is second with 17 pounds (7.8 kilos), then Britain with 16½ pounds (7.5 kilos), Germany with 15½ pounds (7 kilos) and, further down the list, France with 11 pounds (5 kilos), and the United States only 8¾ pounds (4 kilos).

In Britain alone this represents an estimated £3 billion ($4.65 billion) a year spent on chocolate and chocolate products, amounting to an average of 120 chocolate bars, 23

Easter eggs of various sizes and a three and a half pound selection box per person!

In terms of quantity and quality, the Swiss and Belgian chocolate industries are justly renowned. The French make some of the best chocolate at the very top of the scale; and tropical countries, where it is frequently necessary to use additives to prevent the chocolate melting, make the worst.

Shapes and forms

Of course chocolate need not be eaten only as simple bars and sweets – it can be put to work as a vital ingredient in many shapes and forms.

Chocolate Moulds

To make the best chocolate moulds, keep some basic principles in mind.

1. Always use good quality *couverture*, with over 32 per cent cocoa butter. Cooking chocolate or other chocolate derivatives will not do.

2. Melting chocolate is an art known as 'tempering', which, done properly, prevents 'bloom' on the finished product, giving it a smoother appearance and texture.

3. Never let water actually touch the *couverture* – a tiny amount can cause irreparable damage.

The finely chopped *couverture* should be melted very gradually, ideally at about 104°F (40°C), in the oven or a bain marie (water bath). Once melted through, pour three quarters of it onto a marble slab, or a cold stainless steel tray. Spread it out with a palette knife to speed the cooling process, and then scrape it back to the middle before it solidifies. Repeat this process several times, ensuring an even mixture with no air bubbles. Once it has achieved the consistency of clotted cream, mix in thoroughly with the remaining melted chocolate. Never use any solidified pieces which may form on the slab or tray. While working with it, keep the *couverture* at a constant temperature of about 86°F (30°C). The moulds themselves should be spotlessly clean and smooth. Allow at least six hours at room temperature for the chocolate to set, and then it should be easy to separate it from the mould by a light tap on the back. Moulds can be bought from good kitchenware shops, and old-fashioned ones are sometimes found in antique shops.

Chocolate Flakes and Curls

Shave a chocolate bar with a sharp knife, and the flakes will curl of their own accord. For more sophisticated, long, thin curls, spread a thin layer of melted chocolate on marble or another smooth surface. Allow to cool, but not to set hard. With a carving knife push the edge gently at a slight angle into the chocolate layer. The curls will rise up in front of it.

Chocolate Leaves

Pick fresh green leaves from the garden (making sure they are not poisonous!) and wash and dry them carefully on a paper towel. Lay the leaves on some foil and coat with a thin layer of chocolate up to, but not over, the edges. Leave the chocolate to set in a cool place, and then carefully peel off the leaves, beginning at the stalk end.

Chocolate Fruit Dips

Many fruits can be dipped in melted chocolate, but particular favourites are cherries, orange segments, strawberries and grapes. Make sure that the fruit is clean and that any unwanted pith is removed first. For many the ultimate indulgence is a chocolate fondue, in which ready-prepared fruit is individually dipped by guests around a table. Care should be taken to keep the chocolate at an even temperature – the spirit lamp of a conventional cheese or meat fondue set may overheat and spoil the chocolate if used continuously.

Recipe for Chocolate Soufflé

Break 7³⁄₁₀oz (240g) of dark chocolate into pieces, and warm slowly with a spoonful of water in a double saucepan. Separate six eggs; put four yolks into a bowl, add 1½oz (40g) of caster (superfine) sugar and whisk until it has whitened and doubled in volume. Add three tablespoons of unsweetened cocoa powder, mix thoroughly, and mix in the chocolate. Beat six egg whites with a pinch of salt until just short of meringue solid, spoon a quarter of the beaten white into the chocolate and mix. Pour in the rest of the egg whites, and fold them in gently with a spatula. Generously butter a soufflé pan, then put in the mixture and level to the top. Place in an oven preheated to Gas 8 (450°F, 230°C), but then immediately bring down the heat to Gas 6 (400°F, 200°C). Cook for about half an hour, never opening the oven while cooking. Serve immediately.

Sir Edmund Hilary was sustained by chocolate as he conquered Mount Everest accompanied by Sherpa Tensing.

Pope Pius V allowed chocolate to be drunk during the Lenten fast because he found it so disgusting that he could not believe that anyone would drink it voluntarily.

Robert Louis Stevenson worked to establish cocoa plantations on Samoa in the East Indies and wrote: 'I only wish somebody would pay me £10 a day for taking care of cacao, and I could leave literature to others.'

Recipe for Bitter Chocolate Cake

Mix two tablespoons of ground coffee into 2fl oz (50ml) of water and slowly melt 7oz (200g) of dark chocolate with this and one tablespoon of cognac in a bain marie (water bath). Allow 5oz (150g) of butter to soften at room temperature, and then work into a creamy consistency with a fork before mixing thoroughly with the warm chocolate. Beat four small eggs and slowly add to ½oz (15g) of flour. Add the grated peel of half an orange to the chocolate mixture and then add this warm mixture to the eggs and flour, mixing well. Fill a pan lined with greased foil and bake at Gas 3 (325°F, 170°C) for 35 minutes. Leave to cool at room temperature before placing in a refrigerator. Remove four hours before serving and cut into thin slices, adding custard or cream according to preference.

Varieties of chocolate

The versatility of chocolate's form is matched by the variations of its taste. There are several different varieties of chocolate, each a particular favourite of many.

Plain chocolate
The classic dark chocolate produced by the method described in this book. It is still the preferred chocolate of connoisseurs.

White chocolate
This is only vaguely related to chocolate, as it contains no cocoa 'liquor'. It is made with cocoa butter, sugar, and milk. While its texture and appearance are very appealing, it has very little chocolate flavour.

Milk Chocolate

The technique for making solid milk chocolate using condensed milk was invented in the 19th century in Switzerland by Henri Nestlé and Daniel Peter. Nowadays milk chocolate is the preferred choice of most people, and as a result of this innovation, together with Lindt's 'conching' process, the Swiss chocolate industry is today world famous.

Mocha

This was often used to describe a chocolate drink mixed with coffee, or coffee-flavoured chocolate sweets. The word is derived from the Red Sea port from where all the world's coffee was once exported. As a result of this coffee was called mocha and the name lives on in coffee-flavoured products.

Chocolate as an aphrodisiac

Long associated with enhanced virility, chocolate has only recently lost its reputation as a potent aphrodisiac. The Peruvian Indians believed in it, as did Emperor Montezuma. The Colonial archbishops worried about the effect it had on their monks, and it was one of the ingredients in that most notorious of aphrodisiacs, 'Spanish Fly'. Madame du Barry, Louis XI's mistress, gave it to her lovers, and Casanova preferred it to champagne. Although chocolate is no longer directly ascribed such powers, contemporary advertising reflects the erotic charge that it still holds for many today.

How to eat chocolate and stay thin

Diets are big business these days, with chocolate usually seen as one of the greatest sins for the calorie counter. Many a would-be dieter has succumbed to the temptations of a box of chocolates, alternating between guilt and indulgence. All is not lost, however, as there is a trend among diet books of the 'food combining' school to take a more enlightened approach to chocolate. On such a diet chocolate is allowed, but only of the very highest quality, preferably containing 70 per cent cocoa solids, and with a low sugar content. However, while these are undoubtedly the most delicious chocolates, they are also the most expensive.

Colonel Montague James, the first Englishman born in Jamaica, took nothing but cocoa or chocolate for the last 30 years of his life. He lived to be 104.

Celebrating chocolate

Many will be familiar with the use of chocolate in Christmas tree decorations or Easter bunnies, but chocolate is in fact the centrepiece of many celebrations and rituals all around the world, both religious and secular. Here are the highlights of the chocolate calendar.

New Year (1 January)
Eastern Europeans make gifts of chocolate pigs, decorated with chimney sweep motifs.

Epiphany (6 January)
In France the Festival of the Three Kings visiting the infant Jesus is celebrated with chocolates in the shape of the protagonists. The child who finds the chocolate Jesus in the celebration cake becomes King for a day.

Valentine's Day (14 February)
The Japanese have elaborated on the Western idea of giving chocolate hearts to loved ones on Valentine's Day. Only girls are allowed to do so on the day itself, with the men reciprocating with white chocolate a month later. On each occasion a gift of chocolate is also given to one's elders out of respect.

Mother's Day (Variable)
In the United States this multi-denominational festival is always best accompanied by the gift of chocolates.

Easter (Variable)

Originally a pagan festival for Eostre, goddess of birth and spring, it has now become fully incorporated into the Christian calendar. At first painted hard-boiled eggs were given as gifts, but, following the invention of moulding, they were replaced by chocolate eggs.

Halloween

(31 October)

This is celebrated in Mexico as 'Day of the Dead' and marked by picnics in graveyards, where chocolate is an essential accompaniment. More prosaically, the ubiquitous Hershey bar is often a common ingredient of the American 'Trick or Treat' tradition.

St Nicholas (6 December)

The Saint's Day for Santa Claus is more important than Christmas itself in many parts of Europe, with gifts of chocolate boots and bishops for well-behaved children.

Chocolate and love

The role of chocolate in love affairs is usually confined to two scenarios. One involves the gentleman giving chocolates to the lady as a token of his passion, and the other, the hapless female victim of a broken romance consoling herself by eating her way through a box of chocolates. There may be more than a little truth to these clichés; chocolate contains phenylethylamine, a substance which stimulates the brain, creating a state of euphoria similar to that of being in love. Our gallant suitor is perhaps seeking to stimulate such feelings in his mistress, while the scorned lady is trying to keep those feelings alive just a little longer.

Index